Wolf-Dieter Wichmann

KARATE BY PICTURES

An Introduction to Kata

W. Foulsham & Co. Ltd.

London • New York • Toronto • Cape Town • Sydney

W. Foulsham & Company Limited
Yeovil Road, Slough, Berkshire SL1 4JH

ISBN 0–572–01420–1

Originally published by Falken Verlag GmbH, Niederhausen/Ts,
West Germany
© 1985/1987 Falken Verlag
This English language edition © W. Foulsham & Co Ltd 1988

Printed in Great Britain at
St Edmunsbury Press, Bury St Edmunds
Translated by Marion Godfrey

CONTENTS

Karate-Do

Karate-Do is a form of Japanese Budo, or martial arts combat sport, which is becoming increasingly popular in the West. Since anybody interested in Kata, the subject of this book, would already have acquired a basic knowledge of Karate, this introduction will be limited to a few essential points only.

Karate-Do is a form of physical training, consisting of three elements: Kihon (basic training), Kumite (partner training, combat) and Kata (advanced indoor 'form' techniques). All three elements are equally important and omitting one or other forms in Karate training is unthinkable.

Mental and spiritual attitudes towards Karate, your opponent and also to yourself are crucial. Gichin Funakoshi, the founder of modern Karate, said that the aim of Karate was the elevation of the spirit and the practice of humility.

Even if transferring the mental and physical properties of Karate from the sport to the character of the participants is difficult, Karate should never be regarded as an exclusively physical training. Good training in the spirit of 'Karate-Do', or the 'way of Karate', should also serve to instil into exponents such moral values as respect for an adversary, self-discipline and humility. The difficulty of converting such noble ideals into practice is universally acknowledged. How little may rub off during training, is a fact which most instructors will have learned to their cost. But it is the striving which, in itself, is the way towards 'do', or the 'way' of Karate and through which the ultimate purpose of Karate training will become clear.

Kata

In Kihon (basic training), the pupil learns the basic tools of Karate. In time, after many hours of practice, the movements should become as smooth as silk and develop into the typical, lightning-quick techniques so characteristic of Karate.

In Kumite (partner training), the pupil is placed in a situation of having to put the techniques learned into practice at just the right moment and in precisely the right sequence. Only now will the techniques learned acquire a practical value. Practising partner training will not only perfect technique, but will also lead to an improvement in sparring.

There is no direct translation for the word 'Kata'. However, the best way of translating it is by the word 'form'. Kata itself represents combat against several opponents, although these are invisible and exist only in the imagination of the exponent and the spectator. The object is total self defence, by a sequence of set attacking or defensive moves. Modern Karate developed as a sport in its current form around the turn of the century, although 'free sparring' as it is known today was not introduced until the 1930s. Before that, the only Kata contests held were aimed at trying to find the best Karateka (exponent of Karate). Perhaps this underlines the importance of Kata as a criterion in judging the degree of Karate expertise.

Depending on the level of training, there are various practice objectives: correct technique, correct breathing, good stance, perfect timing or rhythm and precision of movement within the spaces marked out in the hall.

There are between 30 and 50 recognised Kata (the number varies according to whether and how many of the different Kata styles are included). In Shotokan Karate, which is the school this book refers to, there are four different groups of Kata (excluding pre-training exercises, such as Taikyo-ku-Kata, which are not dealt with here):

Group 1: Heian 1–5, Tekki 1 or basic Kata elementary grade

Group 2: Bassai-Dai, Jion, Empi, Kanku-Dai, Hungetsu or advanced Kata up to Master grade

Group 3: Bassai-Sho, Kanku-Sho, Jitte, Mekyu, Sochin, etc. or First Grade Master Kata

Group 4: Unsu, Gojushiho-Dai, Gojushiho-Sho or special Kata for Grand Masters and Kata specialists

Every level of training has its own set Kata forms. This also explains why an advanced Kata performed by an elementary grade pupil will always be marked down. Advanced Kata demands the absolute precision of movement and perfection of rhythm which a relative novice cannot possibly have attained.

For this reason, our golden rule is:

Better a perfect lower-grade Kata
Than a mediocre advanced Kata!

Basic Kata is aimed at elementary training objectives, such as the development of a firm stance, good defence and confident movements.

The more advanced Kata forms, of which Empi is a perfect example, promote the development of lightning-quick movements and a rich variety of reflex responses. The simpler forms of basic Kata came about because advanced Kata, once the only form of Kata in existence, proved to be too difficult for the beginner, so the original Kata forms were broken down into their individual components. In this connection, it is interesting to note that Funakoshi speaks of three years in terms of the period required to master a single Kata. Even if a Kata demonstration appears to be successful after several weeks' intensive training, 'mastery' in the true sense of Karate will still be light-years away.

Instructions for Practice

The following approach is the best way of learning Kata forms:

First practise the general sequence of movements, following the step-by-step illustrations (Embu-sen). At this stage, strength, speed and rhythm are not important and the finer points of technique are also irrelevant. When you have mastered the general sequence, the other points should be added. You should then start to develop the technique for timing the holding and relaxing of a position and the fast or slow speed sequences demanded by Kata in its most profound sense. To those lacking a deeper understanding of the meaning of Kata itself, it will probably always remain a mere striking of balletic poses. In good Kata demonstrations, the significance of the movements should become clear, even to the layman.

Etiquette requires that Kata always commences with a formal standing 'greeting'. Put your heels together (Musubi-Dachi), your hands flat on your thighs and bow from the waist. Look straight ahead. This symbolises the dignity and respect which a Karateka should show in the practice of his martial art. After the greeting, you should be in Shizentai position, or 'ready stance' with Hachiji-Dachi, or your feet vertically below your shoulders. The Karateka is now in Zanshin, representing a state of readiness for imminent action.

Every Kata begins with a basic defensive action. This is intended to demonstrate the peaceful nature of training, which has no aggressive purpose, but which, on the contrary, is based on total control. Kata always commences with a glance at the opponent, followed by the opening movements, which should lead swiftly and powerfully, but without haste, into the new stance. Every movement should end with the muscles tightly contracted (Kime), although the tension should be maintained for varying periods of time. These periods may be very brief, as in the 8th movement of the 1st Kata (left Age-Uke) or the 2nd movement of the 2nd Kata (Nagashi-Uke with Ura-Ken), or they may be of normal length, as in the 2nd movement of the 1st Kata (Oi-Zuki) or the 1st movement of the 2nd Kata (double arm block), or the tension may be maintained for very long periods indeed (as in every Kiai).

The symbols accompanying the illustrations give the various Kime times in which tension should be maintained. The key to these is as follows:

◀ keep tension as short as possible

■ hold tension briefly (for just under 1 second)

▰ hold tension normally (for about 1 second)

▰𝕜 hold tension for maximum period (approx. 2 seconds with Kiai)

⌣ transition fluid, without tension

⌢◀ slow, gradual increase in tension as movement develops over about 3 seconds, but with tension held at the end for 1 second

✧ indicates Kiai

The larger photographs, which are numbered to show the particular sequence of movements in the Kata, show the individual movements making up the sequence (e.g. pages 14–22). These are taken from the front, i.e., as seen by a spectator facing the exponent at the start of the Kata. This means that, when we say 'as seen from the left' we mean the *spectator's* left. Some of the larger photographs are accompanied by smaller pictures which explain the reason for the particular movement or show the movements from different angles.

At the end of the Kata the sequence is repeated in a short series of smaller photographs and in a step-by-step diagram (e.g. pages 23–25). The step-by-step diagram (Embu-sen) gives only a rough outline of the positioning of the Kata. For the sake of clarity, we have 'staggered' the stances adopted repeatedly, so that the starting and finishing points do not coincide on these diagrams.

Below is a summary of everything described so far.

Essential Points in Kata Training

- Kata training demands perfectly controlled movement sequences.

- Each technique must be perfect and deliberate, separated by long pauses and purposeful withdrawal movements.

- Rhythm is the 'soul' of Kata. The spirit of Kata springs to life in the characteristic changes of speed from fast to slow, in the focusing and relaxing of muscular tension, in the sudden change from gentle breathing to an explosive exhalation, ending in the power of Kiai, or the harmony of resolve between mind and body.

- Kata is combat! Every movement is adapted to a specific situation. Only those who can identify the situation (attack), who can fight against it, who can 'read' an opponent and his technique and react accordingly, are true exponents of Kata.

- Kata means 'form'. This is reflected by the importance given to the formal sequence of approach, greeting, addressing, concentration and commencement, to starting and ending at the same point, to Zanshin— withdrawal from the final position and the concluding greeting.

Kata 1:
HEIAN SHODAN

Explanatory notes

The 1st Kata is intended to acquaint pupils with the basic terms of Kata. The emphasis here is on clear, generous techniques, taking care not to perform the Kata too quickly. The pupil should start to develop a 'feel' for the space in which Kata combat takes place.

The Hammerfist (4th period) is shown only in its larger form, i.e. as defence against an opponent gripping with both hands. There is also a smaller form, aimed at releasing a one-handed grip, in which the foot is placed in full Zenkutsu-Dachi, or forward stance. When practising the Kata we recommend that anybody below yellow belt grade does not open the hand before the Age-Uke: many novices unconsciously react by opening both hands in an uncontrolled movement. Later on, it will not be difficult simultaneously to stretch and open the hand in a controlled action.

This Kata has 21 positions (periods) and should be performed in about 40 seconds.

Opening position after greeting.
Shizentai in Hachiji-Dachi

Turn to the left in
Zenkutsu-Dachi and execute
Gedan-Barai

①

Explanation:

*Mae-Geri attack deflected by
Gedan-Barai*

Counter-attack with right Oi-Zuki
in Zenkutsu-Dachi

②

Explanation:

Counter-attack

Turning from Oi-Zuki to Gedan-Barai

Right Gedan-Barai in Zenkutsu-Dachi (for explanation see period 1)

③

Tettsui-Uchi 'Hammerfist' in slightly shortened stance

④

Explanation:

Releasing two-handed grip by pulling free and counter-attacking

Counter-attack using Oi-Zuki in Zenkutsu-Dachi

⑤

Turn to the left in Zenkutsu-Dachi with Gedan-Barai

⑥

Block Jodan attack using Age-Uke with edge of hand at the start of the sequence

Explanation:

Grip attacker with left arm and deflect the arm using a right Age-Uke

Right Age-Uke in Zenkutsu-Dachi

⑦

(8)

Right Age-Uke in
Zenkutsu-Dachi with Kiai
Tension should be maintained
for considerably longer than in
the other techniques

(9)

Left Age-Uke in Zenkutsu-Dachi.
Although the tension is held
briefly only and the transition to
the next position should be kept
fluid, do not 'blur' the
movements

Left Gedan-Barai in
Zenkutsu-Dachi

Turn from Age-Uke to left
Gedan-Barai. Make sure stance
is vertical to shoulders

(10)

Right Oi-Zuki in Zenkutsu-Dachi

Turn with right Gedan-Barai in
Zenkutsu-Dachi

Left Oi-Zuki in Zenkutsu-Dachi

Same position,
seen from
right

(14)

Turn with left Gedan-Barai in
Zenkutsu-Dachi

Attack with left
Oi-Zuki in
Zenkutsu-Dachi

Attack with right
Oi-Zuki in
Zenkutsu-Dachi

(15)

(16)

Above
position, seen
from right

Above
position, seen
from right

Attack using right Oi-Zuki with Kiai in Zenkutsu-Dachi Extremely powerful focusing of tension, with stance held for some time

Same position, seen from right

17

Transition to turn executing Shuto-Uke in Kokutsu-Dachi. Turn head at once, making sure final Kokutsu-Dachi position is correctly aligned and weight is mainly on back leg

Explanation:

Deflect using
Shuto-Uke in left
Kokutsu-Dachi

*Chudan Oi-Zuki attack, deflected from
inside, using left Shuto-Uke*

Counter-attack using right
Shuto-Uchi (or deflect with right
Shuto-Uke) in Kokutsu-Dachi.
Stance should be 45° to the
floor

Explanation:

*Counter-attack one opponent using
Shuto-Uchi and deflect attack from
second opponent (not shown here)
coming from right*

Deflect using right Shuto-Uke in
Kokutsu-Dachi
(explanation as on p. 21)

Counter-attack or deflection
using Shuto-Uchi or Shuto-Uke
in right Kokutsu-Dachi.
Stance should be 45° to the
floor
(explanation as on p. 21)

Final Shizentai stance in
Hachiji-Dachi, maintaining
Zanshin (i.e. approx. 3 seconds
in 'ready' position, without
relaxing stance)

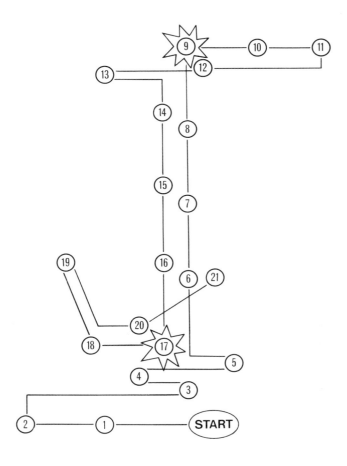

Step-by-step diagram (Embu-sen) of 1st Kata. To make the drawing clearer, the starting and finishing points are not the same (as previously stated). The star symbol indicates Kiai

The 21 positions making up the 1st Kata

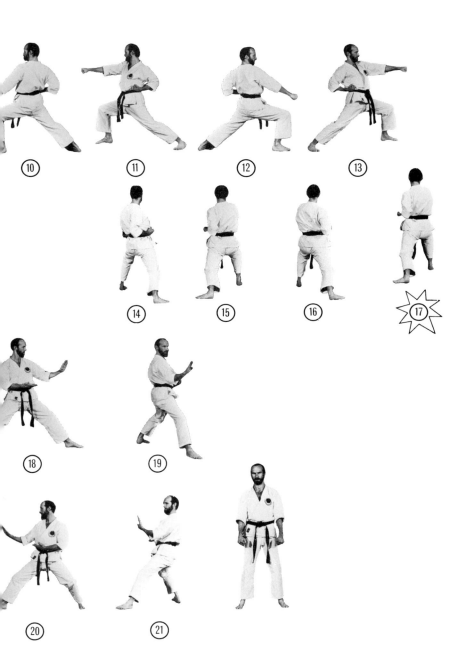

Kata 2:
HEIAN NIDAN

Explanatory notes

The 2nd Kata differs distinctly from the 1st Kata in its degree of difficulty. Techniques performed balancing on one leg, several techniques which must be performed in the same position, as well as counter (Gyaku) techniques, make further demands on the exponent.

Changing position from Zenkutsu-Dachi to Kokutsu-Dachi is more marked, whilst numerous foot techniques have been added.

The first techniques in Kokutsu-Dachi and the reverse combinations with Mae-Geri are the most difficult to master. To improve your stance and body balance, first practise these techniques in front of a mirror.

The Kata must be performed cleanly and deliberately, even though the rhythm will be decidedly more complex and distinctive than in any previously encountered sequence.

There are 26 positions in the Kata, which should be performed in 40 seconds.

Shizentai opening position in Hachiji-Dachi

Jodan double arm block in Kokutsu-Dachi. Take the left arm back until the attack passes the head. The right arm should be against the forehead

①

Explanation:

Block attack from left to the side with Jodan-Oi-Zuki

Explanation:

Deflecting and counter-attacking the same opponent with Jodan-Gyaku-Zuki

②

Simultaneous defence and counter-attack. The left arm deflects the attack past the chin, using Nagashi-Uke: at the same time, the right arm performs a Tettsui-Uchi blow to the elbow (Hammerfist)

Uke-Zuki with a left in Kokutsu-Dachi. Uke-Zuki deflects a Chudan attack and itself has the effect of Chudan-Zuki (see below)

Explanation:

Chudan-Kizami-Zuki attack from the left, Uke-Zuki defence with counter-attack

Explanation to detail:

The attack is blocked to the side by turning the elbow in Tsuki

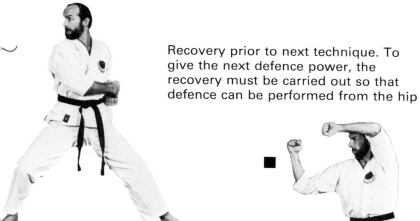

Recovery prior to next technique. To give the next defence power, the recovery must be carried out so that defence can be performed from the hip

Jodan double arm block in Kokutsu-Dachi to the right

④

⑤

⑥

Simultaneous Nagashi-Uke with Tettsui-Uchi (for explanation see 2nd period)

Right Uke-Zuki in Kokutsu-Dachi

29

Recovery into Yoko-Geri.
Reasons for pulling back left leg: to
support the centre of gravity and give
balance for the Yoko-Geri kick. Feet
should be about 30 cm (12 in) apart

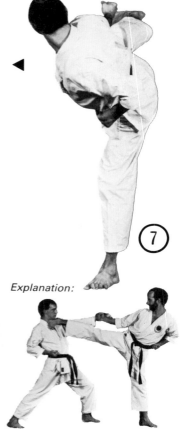

⑦

Yoko-Geri-Jodan with Ura-Ken
right. The Yoko-Geri kick is
performed somewhere between
Keage and Kekomi. Do not
perform too fast, so as to
obscure the effect and do not
hold too long, otherwise the
flow of the Kata will be
interrupted

Explanation:

*Simultaneous deflection of
Jodan-Oi-Zuki with Uraken and
counter-attack using Yoko-Geri*

Same position as above, seen
from the left

Shuto-Uke starting movement. Recovery from Yoko-Geri should start early — whilst still in the air (be careful not to fall over!) — so that you can move smoothly into Shuto-Uke. Bend the knee after the Yoko-Geri, so that you can move into your starting and defence movements

The same movement as above, seen from the left

(8)

Shuto-Uke defence in left Kokutsu-Dachi

Shuto-Uke in right
Kokutsu-Dachi

⑨

Shuto-Uke in left
Kokutsu-Dachi

⑩

⑪

Transition from Shuto-Uke to
Nukite. The front hand makes a
defensive movement and the
hand at the back performs a
Nukite punch from stomach
height, without raising the arm.
Take care not to raise the hips

Nukite in Zenkutsu-Dachi with
Kiai. The left arm, which has
deflected the attack, supports
the right arm — palm
downward — below the elbow

Position 11 seen from the left

Explanation:

The attacker's Oi-Zuki is deflected downwards using Otoshi-Uke

Explanation:

Nukite punch follows the attack which was deflected

Shuto-Uke in left Kokutsu-Dachi. Recovery and explanation as for the same techniques in the 1st Kata

Shuto-Uke in right Kokutsu-Dachi. Body position at 45° to ground

Shuto-Uke in right Kokutsu-Dachi

Shuto-Uke in left Kokutsu-Dachi. Body position at 45° to ground

Recovery movement into right Gyaku-Uchi-Ude-Uke

The old form of this movement, where a Gedan-Haito-Uke was performed by the right hand against Mae-Geri, is no longer practised

Position 16, seen from the left

(16)

Explanation:

Right Gyaku-Uchi-Ude-Uke in Zenkutsu-Dachi. Remember hip movement is crucial here: especially forward and twisting actions

Chudan-Oi-Zuki attack deflected

Right Mae-Geri
Chudan. Pull down
in Gyaku-Zuki and
make sure that the
Mae-Geri snatch
back is crisp

(17)

The technique seen from the
left

Explanation:

Mae-Geri attack
deflected

Technique below seen from the
left

Explanation:

(18)

Left Gyaku-Zuki in
Zenkutsu-Dachi

Adding a Gyaku-Zuki counter-attack to
the Mae-Geri

Recovery
movement into
Gyaku-Uchi-Ude-Uke

There are two forms: the one in
current practice involves
strongly pushing the hip
forwards and downwards in the
Uchi-Ude-Uke. The old form,
which nevertheless remains
viable, meant that the front leg
was pulled back slightly by the
swing of the twisting hip
movement. The important (and
difficult) point to remember is
that the pull back should be
solely the result of hip action,
and not an artificially created
effect!

Position below seen from the
left

Explanation:

A new opponent attacks and is repelled
before the next counter-attack

Left Gyaku-Uchi-Ude-Uke in
Zenkutsu-Dachi

The rhythm of the Kata dictates that this techique should precede
the Mae-Geri. The old form — where it is added on to the
Gyaku-Zuki — is meaningless

37

Explanation of the techniques is the same as on pages 17 and 18

The technique seen from the left

Explanation:

Counter-attacking a previously repelled opponent

Left Mae-Geri Chudan

The technique below seen from the left

Explanation:

Subsequent counter-attack on the same opponent

Right Gyaki-Zuki in Zenkutsu-Dachi

Recovery movement
into the
Morote-Uchi-Ude-Uke

The movement seen from the
left

The position
seen from the
left

Explanation:

*A very strong (heavy) adversary is
repelled by Uchi-Ude-Uke with support
from the other hand*

Right Morote-Uchi-Ude-Uke in
Zenkutsu-Dachi. This technique
has power and speed, to almost
the same degree as a Kiai. The
left fist punches with the base
of the palm, not with the
knuckles. As in all defence
positions, the hip should be
rotated to a 45° angle (Hanmi)

Left Gedan-Barai in Zenkutsu-Dachi defence. Do not open the Zenkutsu-Dachi out too much, since the next movement requires a 45° position

The explanation of the following techniques is as for the 1st Kata

Proceed in Age-Uke. This blocks your opponent, making it possible to break the arm hold using Age-Uke.

Right Age-Uke in Zenkutsu-Dachi, with the body at a 45° angle to the ground

Swivel into right Gedan-Barai defence in Zenkutsu-Dachi

Procedure with pre-blocking

Age-Uke in left Zenkutsu-Dachi, using Kiai. Body should be at 45° angle to ground

Final position in Shizentai

The 26 positions of
the 2nd Kata

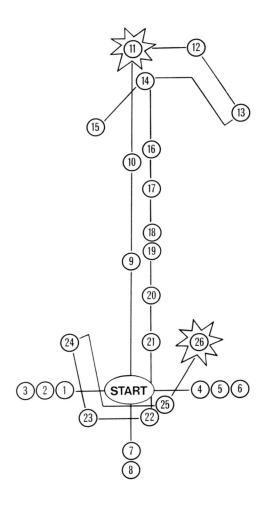

Step-by-step diagram of the 2nd
Kata sequence (for explanation,
see 1st Kata, page 23)

Kata 3:
HEIAN SANDAN

Explanatory notes

The 3rd Kata adds a new position — Kiba-Dachi — which is used extensively from the start. Experience has shown that most Karatekas find it a little difficult at first, so training and meticulous application are extremely important.

In other words: if you perform the Kiba-Dachi in this Kata badly, you have not met one of the essential requirements of this Kata.

The 3rd Kata demands many small, unaccustomed movements and unusual technique combinations, which add further to the difficulty in performing it. This Kata can be approached only with a great deal of effort and devotion, as the text will show.

It is particularly recommended for smaller Karateka, who may perform it as Tokui-(Kur)-Kata.

This Kata comprises 20 positions, which should be performed in approximately 38 seconds.

Opening position in Shizentai with Hachiji-Dachi

Left Uchi-Ude-Uke defence in Kokutsu-Dachi

Explanation:

Side view of the Tate-Shuto-Uke seen from the left

Explanation:

Rise and stretch the right arm (without Kime) to produce a double block, left Uchi-Ude-Uke and right Gedan-Uke

An opponent who attacks with a double fist punch is repelled at the same time. This defence can be used against 2 opponents attacking simultaneously

Recovery movement to next technique. In order to defend, this movement is imperative: in this case it means that the elbows of both arms almost come together before the next double block is performed. The arm which moves upwards (Uchi-Ude-Uke) in the defensive movement moves on the outside, whilst the Gedan-Uke arm moves downwards on the inside

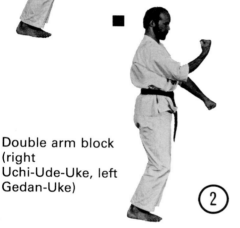

Double arm block (right Uchi-Ude-Uke, left Gedan-Uke)

②

The technique opposite seen from the right

Recovery movement prior to next block

③

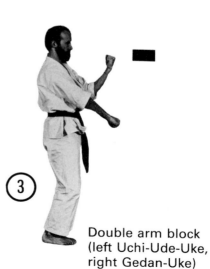

Double arm block (left Uchi-Ude-Uke, right Gedan-Uke)

Rise and stretch the
left arm (no Kime)
into the double
block

Uchi-Ude-Uke in right
Kokutsu-Dachi

Double block (as in period 3)

Double block (as in period 2)

Recovery movement into Morote-Uchi-Ude-Uke. (To give your defence power, go into the recovery movement quickly whilst standing)

The movement opposite seen from the left

Left Morote-Uchi-Ude-Uke in Kokutsu-Dachi

The position seen from the left

Proceed from the recovery (defence) movement to Nukite (explained under position 11 of the 2nd Kata)

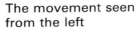

The movement seen from the left

Counter-attack using right Nukite in Zenkutsu-Dachi

The technique seen from the left

Beginning the rotating movement into Tettsui-Uchi

The movement seen from the left

Continuing the turning movement. The left arm moves out of the bent elbow position and moves into Tettsui-Uchi

⑨

The technique seen from the left

Tettsui-Uchi left in Kiba-Dachi

See next page for explanation

*Explanation of Tettsui-Uchi technique
(position 9)*

The opponent in a
double-handed grip on the
preceding Nukite technique

The opponent pulls the arm. (To
understand the movement it is
important that this action is
taken by the opponent!) The
defender starts to turn his own
arm in the direction of the
opposing pull, into the
opponent

Sustaining the turn, the
defender recovers into a
Tettsui-Uchi counter-attack

Final phase: the defender has
turned right around the attacker
and carried out a counter-attack.
Whether or not the defender
has managed to free himself
from his opponent's grip is
unimportant

Counter-attack Oi-Zuki in Zenkutsu-Dachi with Kiai!

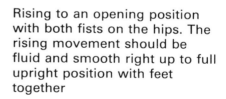

Rising to an opening position with both fists on the hips. The rising movement should be fluid and smooth right up to full upright position with feet together

The technique seen from the left

Repelling a Jodan-Oi-Zuki with
a right Mikazuki-Geri

This form of defence was
introduced to us by Kanazawa.
It is also possible to use the
simpler form, which requires no
prior defensive movement, and
by simply lifting the foot, move
straight into the Fumikomi
stamp

Explanation:

*An opponent attacks by punching and is
repelled by a side kick from the sole of
the foot*

Note: all three pictures are seen from the left

After Mikazuki-Geri the foot is pulled back further, whilst the body moves downwards

In the last phase of the movement downwards, the foot slams down to the floor very quickly in a stamping movement

At the same time as the move downwards in Kiba-Dachi with the foot stamp (Fumikomi-Geri), the elbows go into Empi-Uke defensive position

Empi-Uke (elbow defence) right in Kiba-Dachi with simultaneous stamping step (Fumikomi)

Explanation:

Defence against a Gyaku-Zuki using the elbows (Empi-Uke)

Explanation:

Tate-Uraken counter-attack

It is essential to carry out the Tate-Uraken with great care, otherwise you may find it difficult to untangle yourself from your opponent's arm!

Right Tate-Uraken in Kiba-Dachi. The Uraken should be immediately snapped back to the hip

The technique seen from the left

Note: the following are techniques 12–13, as per the explanation given, but seen from the side

Left Mikazuki-Geri

Step down in Kiba-Dachi with Fumikomi and simultaneous left Empi-Uke

Left Tate-Uraken in Kiba-Dachi

Note: the following are
techniques 12–13, as per
explanation given, but seen
from the left

Right Mikazuki-Geri

(16)

Move down in Kiba-Dachi with
Fumikomi and simultaneous
right Empi-Uke

(17)

Right Tate-Uraken in Kiba-Dachi

The recovery movement into
Tate-Shuto-Uke. It can be carried out in this
form, or over the arm or without using the
left arm at all.
The recovery movement starts fast until it is
under the arm, then moving slowly, but with
increasing tension, to its close

Side view of recovery
movement seen from the left

Explanation:

Right Tate-Shuto-Uke in
Kiba-Dachi

Repelling an Oi-Zuki from inside

Counter-attack using left Oi-Zuki in Zenkutsu-Dachi. By adding pre-technique tension, the Oi-Zuki can become very powerful

Side view of left Oi-Zuki

Turning from the Oi-Zuki in Zenkutsu-Dachi into double punch with Jodan-Mawashi-Zuki (right) and Chudan-Ushiro-Empi (left) in Kiba-Dachi

For the turn, bring the right foot forward towards the left foot in a vertical line with the shoulder. Then pivot around the right foot and turn into Kiba-Dachi

Explanation:

An opponent holds the defender in a double arm hold from behind

The defender slips down into the lower position of the Kiba-Dachi, at the same time counter-attacking to the head and stomach

Jodan-Mawashi-Zuki (left) double punch and Chudan-Ushiro-Empi (right) in Kiba-Dachi with Kiai! The punch should be carried out to the right whilst sliding in Kiba-Dachi position. The sliding movement should start by a shift to the left leg, i.e. the right leg moves first

20

Final position in Shizentai

The 20 positions of the 3rd Kata

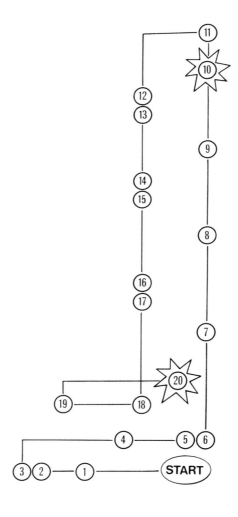

Step-by-step diagram of the 3rd
Kata sequence (see 1st Kata,
page 23, for explanation)

Kata 4:
HEIAN YONDAN

Explanatory notes

The 4th Kata is one of the most difficult in the Heian series. Whilst the 5th Kata, which is next, is dominated by powerful, explosive fighting techniques, which most serious Kata exponents find relatively easy to perform, the 4th Kata demands an elegance and lightness of touch to produce a demonstration of technical excellence.

The characteristic features of this Kata are: repeated changes from Kokutsu-Dachi to Zenkutsu-Dachi and transition from the slower techniques where the build up of tension is gradual, to the more explosive, powerful techniques.

Only meticulous control of the rhythm and correct focus of tension will enable a Karateka to perform this Kata well.

The Kata contains 27 positions and should be performed in about 45 seconds.

Opening position Shizentai in Hachiji-Dachi

Recovery movement to double block: this is a sideways Gedan deflection: quick, but without Kime

Explanation:

Repelling Jodan-Oi-Zuki from the side, with simultaneous recovery movement of the right hand (e.g. for Shuto-Uchi)

Double block with Haishu-Uke (left arm) and Jodan-Kamae (or Age-Uke) (right arm) in Kokutsu-Dachi. After a quick recovery movement, the defensive movement follows slowly and smoothly, breathing in for about 3 seconds. The conclusion is a strong focus of tension, but take care that movements are not jerky!

Recovery movement into double block

Double block (as in period 1) in Kokutsu-Dachi

Explanation:

The defender must go into Mae-Geri attack very quickly and powerfully, which is why there is no separate recovery movement

Recovery movement to Gedan-Juji-Uke. Hands move directly down from the double block into the Juji-Uke

Explanation:

The Mae-Geri attack must be blocked before the attacking leg is stretched!

Defence using Gedan-Juji-Uke in Zenkutsu-Dachi

③

The technique seen from the left

Recovery into
Morote-Uchi-Ude-Uke

Explanation:

*Block Morote-Uchi-Ude-Uke with
Chudan-Oi-Zuki attack*

Defence with
Chudan-Morote-Ude-Uke in
right Kokutsu-Dachi

④

69

Recovery into Yoko-Geri. Pull the left leg forward sharply to standing position, before raising it into the Yoko-Geri. At the same time, swing the hands around towards the right hip and keep your head turned towards your opponent

Explanation:

An opponent using Jodan-Oi-Zuki to attack is repelled with Uraken and at the same time attacked with a Yoko-Geri.

Jodan-Yoko-Geri with Chudan-Uraken. First snap back the Yoko-Geri, then open the hand, finishing with Empi (see the following pictures).
(Either Keage or Kekomi: compare text on 7th position in 2nd Kata)

Gyaku-Mae-Empi counter-attack
in Zenkutsu-Dachi

Pull back movement after
Yoko-Geri to move into Empi.
Open left fist in preparation for
the Empi

Yoko-Geri with right Uraken (as
in position 6)

Straightening up and recovery
movement for right Yoko-Geri

Left Gyaku-Mae-Empi counter-attack in Zenkutsu-Dachi

(10)

Side view of Empi with right hand in front, seen from left

Side view of recovery movement seen from left

Explanation:

A (very low) Chudan-Mae-Geri is blocked to the side

Gedan-Shuto-Uke defence, going into recovery movement taking the palm of the right hand to the back of the head. In the slower European form, the tension is held for a short time after the movement. In its Japanese form, Gedan-Shuto-Uke flows directly into the next movement. Both forms are acceptable

Simultaneous counter-attack using Jodan-Shuto-Uchi and Age-Uke (with open hand) defence in Zenkutsu-Dachi

(11)

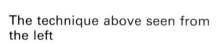

The technique above seen from the left

Explanation:

After the Mae-Geri attack the opponent will withdraw with a Jodan-Oi-Zuki. He is repelled with Age-Uke, and counter-attacked with Shuto-Uchi. The upper body which is facing directly ahead will be at a different angle from the Zenkutsu-Dachi position (45° left forward)

Counter-attack using Mae-Geri

⑫

Side view of Mae-Geri

Explanation:

The counter-attack is executed with Mae-Geri-Chudan

When pulling back from the Mae-Geri, an attack is deflected downwards by the palm of the left hand, whilst the right hand continues on above the head into Uraken

Side view of above movement

Explanation:

Simultaneous repelling of a Chudan-Zuki with recovery into Uraken

75

Counter-attack using Chudan-Uraken in
Kosa-Dachi with Kiai! (Kosa-Dachi: the
right foot should point straight ahead,
with the left foot at a 45° angle behind
and the left knee touching the right calf.)

Side view of
Uraken

Explanation:

*Move in towards your
opponent using
Chudan-Uraken*

Recovery movement into
Kakiwake-Uke. Go into the
movement briskly, but without
haste. Body position should be
45° to the ground

Explanation:

*The defender is attacked from the rear
(stranglehold) and moves between the
arms of the attacker with arms crossed*

Explanation:

*Push the attacker far enough back until
you can counter-attack with a Mae-Geri*

Kakiwake-Uke in left
Kokutsu-Dachi. Defence
deflected outwards after about 3
seconds. Twist the forearms
outwards (inside arm turned
away from the body) from the
recovery position (inside arms
turned towards face)

Right Mae-Geri-Keage

The same technique seen from
the front

Explanation:

*Use a Mae-Geri to attack an opponent
who has been repelled by a block*

Step back with right Choku-Zuki in
Zenkutsu-Dachi. (No recovery into Tsuki
— punch carried out immediately after the
Kakiwake-Uke)

Gyaku-Zuki in
stance
(Zenkutsu-Dachi)

⑯

⑰

Transition to
recovery
movement into
Kakiwake-Uke,
45° to ground

⑱

Right Kakiwake-Uke in
Kokutsu-Dachi

79

Left Mae-Geri-Keage

(19)

(20)

Stepping back with left
Choku-Zuki in
Zenkutsu-Dachi

(21)

Gyaku-Zuki in stance
(Zenkutsu-Dachi)

Transition from Kokutsu-Dachi with recovery into Morote-Uchi-Ude-Uke

The movement opposite seen from the right

22

Left Morote-Uchi-Ude-Uke in Kokutsu-Dachi

The technique seen from the right

81

Right
Morote-Uchi-Ude-Uke in
Kokutsu-Dachi

The technique seen from
the right

(23)

(24)

Left Morote-Uchi-Ude-Uke in
Kokutsu-Dachi

The technique seen from the
right

Transition with leading foot to
Zenkutsu-Dachi. At the same time, stretch
the open hands to the head (on no
account open hands wider than the width
of the head).
In the Japanese form the foot does not
move into Zenkutsu-Dachi and only the
back leg is stretched into Zenkutsu-Dachi

The technique seen
from the right

Explanation:

*After repelling the attack, grip your
opponent's head with both hands*

Counter-attack using right Hiza-Geri
with Kiai! Moving downwards
sharply, the open hands close into
fists, stopping just below the knee

The technique seen from
the right

Explanation:

*Slam your opponent's head down onto
your knee*

Step back into the Shuto-Uke

Left Shuto-Uke in
Kokutsu-Dachi

26

Right Shuto-Uke
in Kokutsu-Dachi

Final position in Shizentai

27

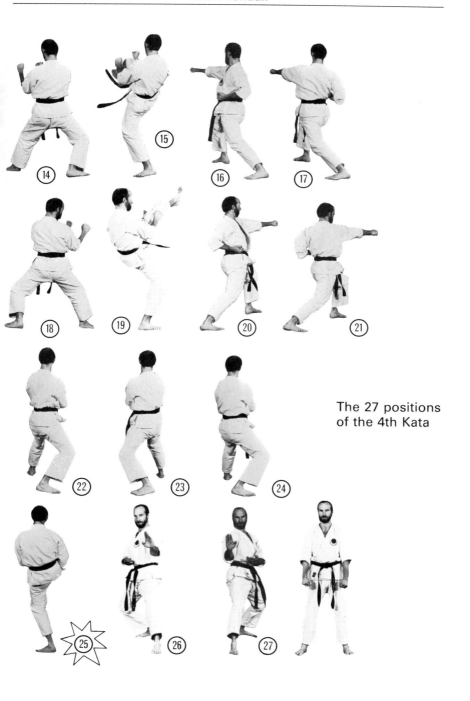

The 27 positions
of the 4th Kata

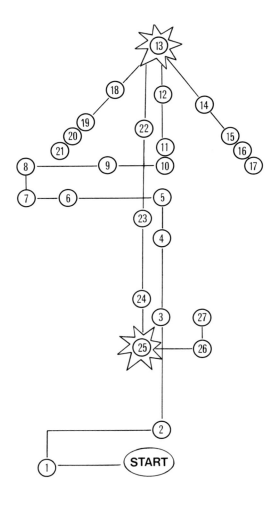

Step-by-step diagram of the 4th
Kata sequence (for explanation
see 1st Kata, page 23)

Kata 5:
HEIAN GODAN

Explanatory notes

The 5th Kata is the last one in the Heian series. It is no less complex and expressive than the next Kata stage, being particularly noted for its balance and harmony. The required elements are not too specialised, which is why it is often selected by exponents for demonstration purposes.

The clarity of its sharply defined rhythms makes it superbly suited to synchronised Kata displays.

Differences in the way in which the form is practised in Europe and Japan are explained in the text.

The Kata has 23 positions and should be performed in 45 seconds.

Opening position Shizentai in
Hachiji-Dachi

Repelling left Uchi-Ude-Uke in
Kokutsu-Dachi

①

Explanation:

*Use Uchi-Ude block to repel the
Oi-Zuki-Chudan attack from the left*

(2)

Counter-attack left
Gyaku-Zuki-Chudan in
Kokutsu-Dachi

Explanation:

Counter-attack using Gyaku-Zuki

Explanation:

(3)

Straighten up into
Heisoku-Dachi, with left
Kagi-Zuki. The movement
should be as liquid as 'flowing
water' in all elements: head,
arms, legs should move
smoothly together. In final
position, your head should be
turned to the right

*Hold your opponent by the shoulder in
a Gyaku-Zuki and throw to the right
against the direction of the
straightening up movement to the left*

Right Uchi-Ude-Uke in Kokutsu-Dachi

④

Right Gyaku-Zuki in Kokutsu-Dachi

⑤

⑥

Straighten up in Heisoku-Dachi with right Kagi-Zuki, looking to the front

Move forwards out of the Heisoku-Dachi in right Morote-Uchi-Ude-Uke in Kokutsu-Dachi

Recovery movement forwards in the Zenkutsu-Dachi, with both arms to the right!

⑦

Gedan-Juji-Uke in Zenkutsu-Dachi seen from the left

⑧

Explanation:

Left Gedan-Juji-Uke in Zenkutsu-Dachi

An opponent blocks a Mae-Geri attack using a Gedan-Juji-Uke

Maintain stance
(Zenkutsu-Dachi) and defend
using Jodan-Juji-Uke with open
hands. Arms should be slightly
bent

(9)

The above technique
seen from the left

Explanation:

*After the Mae-Geri attack the opponent
follows through with Jodan-Oi-Zuki and
is blocked*

Transition to defensive movement

The technique seen from the left

Explanation:

Osae-Uke in Zenkutsu-Dachi. Both hands should be placed flat on top of each other at right angles and slammed downwards to repel an attack

An opponent moving back in Chudan-Gyaku-Zuki stance is repelled downwards

Tate-Shuto-Uke deflection moving
forwards. The Japanese form uses a
Chudan-Zuki instead of a Tate-Shuto-Uke.
Both forms are possible here

Tate-Shuto-Uke
seen from the
left

⑪

Explanation:

*Whilst moving forward to
counter-attack, a further Tsuki is
repelled*

Explanation:

⑫

Closing attack using Oi-Zuki

Oi-Zuki-Chudan in
Zenkutsu-Dachi with Kiai!

Recovery movement into stamping step (Fumikomi) with simultaneous Gedan-Barai deflection

Recovery movement seen from the left

Moving down with Fumikomi and Gedan-Barai in Kiba-Dachi seen from the left

Explanation:

Fumikomi and right Gedan-Barai in Kiba-Dachi

At the same time as repelling your opponent's Oi-Zuki attack, counter-attack with Fumikomi to the instep of the foot

Recovery movement into
Chudan-Heishu-Uke. Move quickly,
turning the head at the same time

Recovery
movement seen
from the left

Chudan-Heishu-Uke
seen from the left

Explanation:

⑭

Left Chudan-Heishu-Uke
in Kiba-Dachi

*Your opponent's Chudan-Oi-Zaki attack
is punched away to the side*

Deflect with right Mikazuki-Geri. (The left hand remains as a 'target' to be hit. It is important *not* to use the hips when performing this movement!)

Mikazuki-Geri seen from the left

Explanation:

Although the opponent is holding the defending arm, a Mikazuki-Geri kick is still carried out, keeping the hips well back

Right Chudan-Mae-Empi in Kiba-Dachi. The left hand provides the target in front of the elbow

Explanation:

From the Mikazuki-Geri, come down into a counter-attack with a Mae-Empi

Explanation:

Repelling a new opponent by going in from the side with Morote-Uchi-Ude-Uke

Chudan-Morote-Uchi-Ude-Uke deflection in Kosa-Dachi (keep the right foot straight and the left at a 45° angle behind, with the left knee touching the right calf). Make sure you maintain the same height going into this movement as for Empi!

■ Counter-attack using Morote-Ura-Zuki in Renoji-Dachi. Look in the opposite direction; your position should also be facing the new opponent

⑱

The technique seen from the left

Explanation:

The defensive movement should be followed by a form of blow to your opponent's chin, bringing you up to establish eye contact with the next opponent

Jump off and recovery movement. Take off from the left leg and slam both fists into the hips in the air. In *one* form, Kiai is maintained

Explanation:

Jump over the stick

Explanation:

The Mae-Geri attack is blocked in the descent

Jump down with Gedan-Juji-Uke. You should be at right angles to the ground. Keep the right leg in front and the left 'kneeling' behind, but without the knee touching the ground. Another form uses Kiai here. Both versions are permissible

Deflect with right
Morote-Uchi-Ude-Uke in
Zenkutsu-Dachi

⟨20⟩

Morote-Uchi-Ude-Uke seen from
the left

Transition movement
into Nukite technique,
using a swift
Gedan-Shuto-Uke
deflection with recovery
movement behind the
head to move into the
Nukite

The transition seen from the left

Explanation:

*When turning to the new opponent, use
a Ushiro-Ashi-Barai to sweep your
opponent aside, at the same time
fending off the attack with a
Gedan-Shuto-Uke*

103

Gedan-Nukite (right) at the same time
as Nagashi- Uke (left) in
Zenkutsu-Dachi.
Instead of the Nukite, carry out a
Shuto-Uchi

(20a)

Nukite seen from the left

Explanation:

*Divert the Jodan-Oi-Zuki attack past the
head of your opponent, then attack
using a Nukite. The attack can take the
form of a blow to the lower body or —
as in this case — it may be carried out
in preparation for the throw*

104

(21)

Transition to Gedan-Barai with left Jodan-Uchi-Ude-Uke in Kokutsu-Dachi.
Do not raise the hip or step back!
In its Japanese form the Zenkutsu-Dachi remains on one line at the outset, to prevent any foot movement at all

The above position seen from the left

When turning, the defender grasps the attacker's leg and throws him to the left

Slowly rise in Heisoku-Dachi, without any movement of the arms

Side view from the left

(22)

Turn on the left heel in Heisoku-Dachi, with simultaneous Gedan-Uke and Uchi-Ude-Uke

Heisoku-Dachi with Gedan-Uke and Uchi-Ude-Uke

Side view

This form, with its short standing pause, is the form most commonly practised in Europe. The Japanese form, in which the exponent moves directly into the Nukite technique, is illustrated on the next page

The Japanese form: move directly from
the turn into the Nukite in Zenkutsu-Dachi

Left Gedan-Nukite and right
Nagashi-Uke in Zenkutsu-Dachi

Explanation:

Nukite seen from
the left

*As in the first case, divert the attack
past the head and prepare for the
throw!*

Gedan-Uke and right
Uchi-Ude-Uke in Kokutsu-Dachi

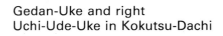

Side view

Final position in Shizentai

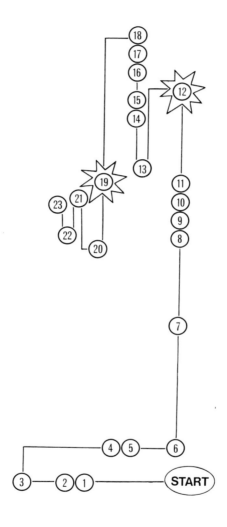

Step-by-step diagram of the 5th
Kata sequence (for explanation,
see 1st Kata, page 23)

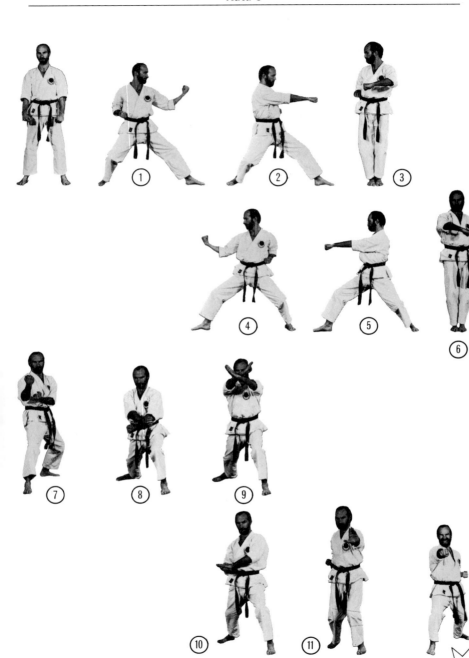

The 23 positions
of the 5th Kata

Kata 6:
TEKKI SHODAN

Explanatory notes

The Tekki Shodan Kata hardly
bears comparison with the
previous Heian series. It is a
very specialised form of training
for the Kiba-Dachi position,
involving relatively difficult
advanced techniques.

Practical experience has shown
that it is virtually impossible to
give a good account of Tekki
using normal training
techniques. Only by intensifying
your efforts and dissecting
every movement will you be
able to do justice to this
particular Kata.

Great care should be taken to
ensure that the *same* hip height
is maintained at all times and
that the hips do not move with
the various techniques being

performed. In keeping with this
level of expertise, many of the
techniques are not linked by
recovery movements. Herein
lies the skill of the expert, who
will demonstrate complete
mastery of the dynamics of the
form without recovery or step
movements.

The direction of the gaze is of
particular importance, since it is
here that many errors creep in.

The Kata begins and ends with
a different opening position and
this is where some mistakes
may crop up. In particular, the
same foot (the right foot)
should be pulled back and
moved forward again.

The Kata has 29 positions and
should be performed in
approximately 40 seconds.

Opening Shizentai position in Hachiji-Dachi

Place the right leg in Kata Tekki 1 opening position in Heisoku-Dachi The right hand should be open below the left (to protect the lower body)

Kosa-Dachi with Nagashi-Uke. Bend the knees slightly, crossing the left foot over the right, but without putting any weight on it. Look to the right and make a defensive movement with both hands to fend off a Mae-Geri from the front

113

Simultaneous recovery into
Fumikomi (stamping step) and
Chudan-Heishu-Uke.
The Fumikomi form introduced by
Kanazawa which uses an
exaggerated recovery movement is
already being replaced by a short,
quicker Japanese form of recovery
movement. Whichever form you use,
it is important to stamp the
Fumikomi *down* from mid-body
height

Explanation:

Chudan-Heishu-Uke with right
Fumikomi in Kiba-Dachi

*Defence coupled with counter-attack to
the instep*

(3)

Maintain stance (Kiba-Dachi) for Mae-Empi (left) to the right against the target of the right and twist the upper body as far as possible without moving the hips

(4)

Maintain stance (Kiba-Dachi) and snap fists down to hips into Kamae. Turn and look left!

(5)

Maintain stance (Kiba-Dachi) and go into defensive move with left Gedan-Uke

Explanation:

Blocking an opponent's Chudan-Oi-Zuki

All techniques should be carried out without any special recovery movements

(6)

Maintain stance
(Kiba-Dachi) for right
Kagi-Zuki

~

(7)

Convert to Kosa-Dachi (without
transferring weight to the right
leg)

Recovery into Fumikomi with
Uchi-Ude-Uke.
During the recovery the left
hand should not leave the hip:
take the leg as high as possible.
Remember to turn your head
and look to the front!

Right
Uchi-Ude-Uke
in Kiba-Dachi

Explanation:

Repelling a frontal attack by an opponent

⑧

Recovery into Gedan-Uke-Zuki
with Jodan-Nagashi-Uke

⑨

Counter-attack with
Ura-Zuki, with support
from the fist of the right
arm under the left elbow

Explanation:

The right hand may carry out a block at the same time as the Ura-Zuki counter-attack

117

Start the next movement by distinctly turning the direction of your gaze

Nami-Gaeshi defending kick

Explanation:

If the arms are blocked, you may use the foot to block a kick

Explanation:

Left Morote-Ude-Uke in Kiba-Dachi. Turn fist with the little finger facing outwards. If you are athletic enough, defend outwards!

After defending with the frontal kick, another opponent, attacking from the side with a Chudan-Oi-Zuki, is repelled

Look round! Deflect with
Nami-Gaeshi and recover into
Morote-Uke

Right Chudan-Morote-Ude-Uke.
Turn fist inwards

Look round! Slam fists down to
hips in Kamae

Left Chudan-Zuki and right
Chudan-Kagi-Zuki in Kiba-Dachi
with Kiai!

Left Haishu-Uke in Kiba-Dachi

Quick recovery into Haishu-Uke

Chudan-Mae-Empi

Turn your head! Slam your fists
down to the hips in Kamae

Right Gedan-Uke in Kiba-Dachi

Left Kagi-Zuki

Step across with left foot in
Kosa-Dachi

Recovery movement into
Fumikomi and Uchi-Ude-Uki.
(Turn and look to the front!)

After Fumikomi-Geri, step straight into Kiba-Dachi and execute Uchi-Ude-Uke to the left

Left Gedan-Uke-Zuki and right Jodan-Nagashi-Uke

Right Ura-Zuki supported by left arm

Turn your head!

Nami-Gaeshi kick right with
recovery into Morote-Ude-Uke

(25)

Right Morote-Ude-Uke. Turn fist
outwards

(26)

(27)

Nami-Gaeshi kick to the left
with recovery into
Morote-Ude-Uke

Left Morote-Ude-Uke. Turn fist
inwards

Turn and look round! Slam fists
down to hips in Kamae

Right Chudan-Zuki with left
Chudan-Kagi-Zuki in Kiba-Dachi
with Kiai!

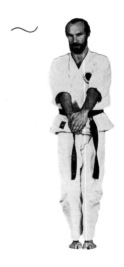

Straighten up into Tekki 1
opening position

Final Shizentai position (move
right leg over)

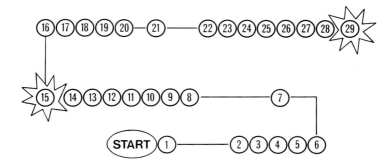

Step-by-step diagram of the 6th
Kata sequence (for explanation
see 1st Kata, page 23)

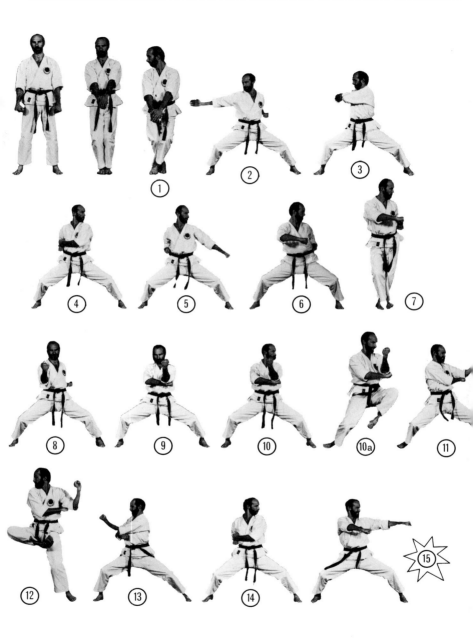

The 29 positions
of the Tekki
Shodan Kata

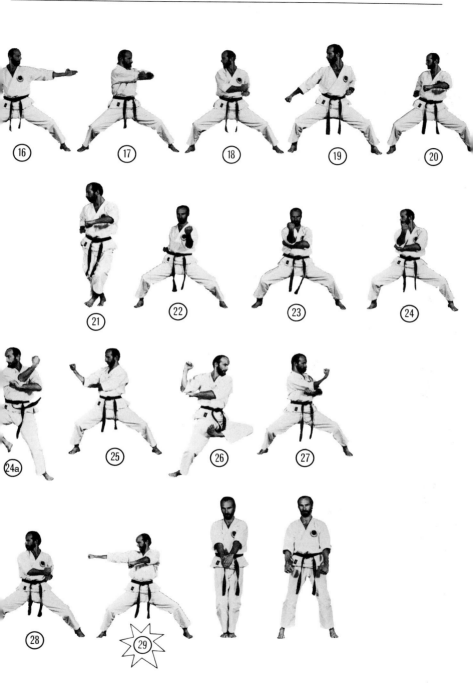

Kata 7:
BASSAI-DAI

Explanatory notes

Bassai-Dai is the last of the Kata forms described in this book. It is correspondingly longer and more demanding than the previous Kata sequences, although in some respects, it hardly exceeds the boundaries of what is required for the normal basic techniques.

Hip work is emphasised by positions which demand a firm stance and good balance.

Bassai-Dai is a Kata for the strong, compact fighter intent on optimising weight and power. Training and practice should focus on sweeping recovery movements and powerful use of the hips.

The Kata has 42 positions and should take about 70 seconds to perform.

Opening Shizentai position in
Hachiji-Dachi

Opening position seen from the
right

Opening stance for the
Bassai-Dai Kata. Step across to
the left foot, place your right fist
in your left palm, keeping your
left thumb on top

129

Recovery movement seen from the right

Recovery movement and jumping step into the Morote-Uchi-Ude-Uke

Morote-Uchi-Ude-Uke seen from the right

①

Explanation:

Right Morote-Uchi-Ude-Uke in Kosa-Dachi.
Cross-over position: right foot should be straight, the left foot should be behind, raised up on the ball at an angle of 45°, with the left knee supporting the right calf. The left hand should be flat against the side of the right elbow

Very strong block, using the whole of the body

Left Uchi-Ude-Uke
seen from the right

(2)

eft Uchi-Ude-Uke in
enkutsu-Dachi

Explanation:

*Deflecting a
Chudan-Oi-Zuki*

Right
Gyaku-Uchi-Ude-
Uke seen from
the right

(3)

Explanation:

Maintain stance
Zenkutsu-Dachi) and
epel Gyaku-Uchi-Ude-Uke

ll these defensive movements
hould be preceded by a
ecovery movement, followed
y turning the hips downwards
r outwards

*Deflecting a Gyaku-Zuki from
the same opponent*

Recovery movement whilst
turning. Extend the right arm in
the new direction, while the left
arm sweeps round

④

Left Gyaku-Soto-Ude-Uke in
Zenkutsu-Dachi

⑤

Uchi-Ude-Uke in Zenkutsu-Dachi

Explanation:

Turn back to the back leg and swivel 90° to the right. Carry out sweeping defence movement, keeping well down

When straightening up, stretch the left arm and sweep into a recovery movement with the right (first version)

A low Mae-Geri attack can be held with a leg hold. In order to throw the opponent backwards off balance, a hard shove or push with the left hand on the opponent's chest is sufficient

Punch forward with closed fist (second version)

Recovery movement without use of left hand (third version)

Step forward in Zenkutsu-Dachi with Soto-Ude-Uke

⑥

⑦

Left Gyaku-Uchi-Ude-Uke in Zenkutsu-Dachi

Explanation:

After the throw a further opponent, attacking with a Tsuki from the left, is repelled

(8)

Straighten up with fist Kamae to right hip.
Previously carried out slowly, this movement should now flow quickly

(9)

Left Tate-Shuto-Uke in Hachiji-Dachi left. An opponent is repelled, held and pulled into the following Tsuki counter-attack

(10)

Right Choku-Zuki in the Hachiji-Dachi

135

Recovery into Uchi-Ude-Uke. The movement should be generous, in keeping with the essence of the Bassai-Dai. Try and follow through under the other arm.

⑪

Uchi-Ude-Uke in a position which is almost transformed into a Zenkutsu-Dachi by swivelling the hips and bending the left knee.
Turn the feet, making sure not to move from the spot

Explanation:

Frontal attack repelled in upright stance. Move left by shifting weight to the left

Left Chudan-Choku-Zuki in
Hachiji-Dachi

Explanation:

Chudan-Choku-Zuki counter-attack

Left Uchi-Ude-Uke, turning back

Recovery into Shuto-Uke. Depending on
Kata style used (Kanazawa = deliberate,
Ochi = rapid), turn the left leg with more
or less speed, before moving the right leg
forwards

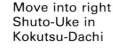
Move into right
Shuto-Uke in
Kokutsu-Dachi

(14)

Move into left
Shuto-Uke in
Kokutsu-Dachi

(15)

Short move with
right Shuto-Uke

(16)

Step back with
left Shuto-Uke in
Kokutsu-Dachi

138

Transition from Kokutsu-Dachi
to Zenkutsu-Dachi with recovery
into Tsukami-Uke

Recovery movement
follow-through

Zenith of the recovery
movement

Explanation:

*It is possible to repel the attack by a
cross-over movement before blocking
the movement downwards*

Tsukami-Uke in Zenkutsu-Dachi. Only the fingertips and thumb of the left hand touch the wrist and forearm of the right hand

Side view

Explanation:

After repelling the attack, the opponent is held in check

Recovery into
Gedan-Yoko-Geri-Kekomi. This
movement should follow
through to between the arms

Side view of the Yoko-Geri

Explanation:

Simultaneous hold with right
Gedan-Yoko-Geri-Kekomi with
Kiai!

*Hold your opponent and attack using a
kick to the hip (or the side of the knee)*

141

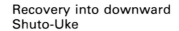

Recovery into downward
Shuto-Uke

Shuto-Uke in
left
Kokutsu-Dachi

Left
Shuto-Uke,
seen from the
left

Step forward
with
Shuto-Uke in
Kokutsu-Dachi

Right
Shuto-Uke,
seen from the
left

142

Lift the arms in Jodan-Morote-Uke in Heisoku-Dachi. Pull the right leg back slowly from the Kokutsu-Dachi Shuto-Uke and move the hand over to the other hand in front of the stomach. When the feet are closed, lift both hands from the chest and straighten up. At the beginning of the movement, the elbows are close to the body, moving apart when the fists are about chin height. The movement closes with the fists reaching the forehead, and the knuckles of the index fingers touching, with elbows wide apart

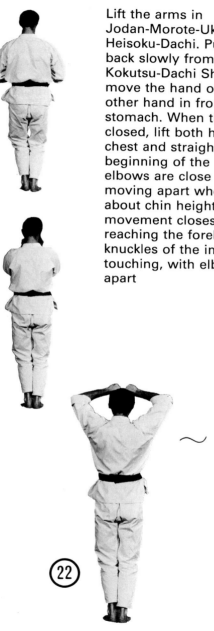

Explanation given on next page

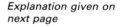

The movement seen from the left

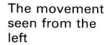

Explanation:

Breaking loose by lifting the arms in Morote-Uke

Breaking loose by snapping arms apart with Hiza-Geri. The Hiza-Geri is not performed in the Japanese form

Hiza-Geri seen from the left

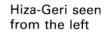

Explanation:

Breaking the hold and counter-attacking with Hiza-Geri

Step into Zenkutsu-Dachi with Hasami-Uchi

Side view of the Hasami-Uchi

Explanation:

After breaking free, the opponent is attacked with a double punch to the lower ribs from both fists

Slide forwards with Yori-Ashi in
Kizami-Zuki-Chudan right

(24)

Side view of the Kizami-Zuki

Explanation:

*Following through
with a closing
technique*

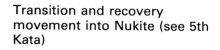

Transition and recovery movement into Nukite (see 5th Kata)

Nukite in Zenkutsu-Dachi

Side view of the Nukite

Slow, crisp straightening up with Gedan-Uke and Jodan-Uchi-Ude-Uke

Side view of stance in Heisoku-Dachi

Recovery movement into Fumikomi with Gedan-Barai

Step into Fumikomi and Gedan-Barai in Kiba-Dachi

Side view of Gedan-Barai

Recovery movement into a rapid Haishu-Uke

Deflect with left Haishu-Uke in Kiba-Dachi

Side view of the Haishu-Uke

Counter-attack using
Mikazuki-Geri

Side view of the
Mikazuki-Geri

Step into Kiba-Dachi with right
Mae-Empi. The left arm is kept
in front of the right arm as a
target

Maintain stance (Kiba-Dachi),
using right Gedan-Uke
deflection without recovery
movement. Keep left fist on the
right elbow with the back of the
hand facing front

Explanation:

The first attacker using Mae-Geri is repelled to the side without moving the body

Side view of right Gedan-Uke

Left Gedan-Uke in Kiba-Dachi. The right fist should be on the left elbow, with the back of the hand facing front

Explanation:

The second attacker is also directly repelled without any change in body position

Transition to Zenkutsu-Dachi with swift Kamae to left hip. In Europe, exponents go directly from the Kiba-Dachi and a short recovery into the Yama-Zuki which follows. The Japanese form allocates a separate period (and pause) for the movement

Right Gedan-Uke in Kiba-Dachi

Side view of the Yama-Zuki

Yama-Zuki in Zenkutsu-Dachi right. A Ura-Zuki blow from the right arm to the stomach, with the left arm to the head in a Jodan-Zuki. The upper Tsuki should be carried out so as to repel a Jodan attack at the same time (keep elbow and fist *aligned* to the front). This explains the diagonal position of the upper body, shoulder and head

151

Explanation:

Simultaneous defensive movement with Jodan and Chudan-Zuki counter-attack

There are 2 possible forms of straightening up in Heisoku-Dachi: straight Heisoku-Dachi, or at a 45° angle. In the case of a straight Heisoku-Dachi, the next attack should be repelled with Mikazuki-Geri (see picture sequence on next page) In the case of the 45° angle Heisoku-Dachi, a Hiza-Geri should be used to repel the attack. This is an important point to remember!

Straighten up with Kochi-Kamae to the right hip and straight Heisoku-Dachi

1st opening
position with
standing
Heisoku-Dachi.
Mikazuki-Geri
defence

Explanation of 1

2nd opening position
with 45° angled
Heisoku-Dachi.
Hiza-Geri defence

Explanation of 2

Left Mikazuki-Geri

Side view of the
Mikazuki-Geri

Left Yama-Zuki in
Zenkutsu-Dachi

Side view of the Yama-Zuki

(36)

Fluid straightening up in
Heisoku-Dachi with
Koshi-Kamae to left

Side view of
the Kamae in
Heisoku-Dachi

Right Mikazuki-Geri

Side view of the Mikazuki-Geri

155

(37)

Step into right Zenkutsu-Dachi
with Yama-Dachi (as in previous
techniques)

90° angle transition to
alignment in Zenkutsu-Dachi.
Start a sweeping recovery
movement

Follow-through of recovery in
Zenkutsu-Dachi under the arm

(38)

Sukui-Uke ('scooping' defence
movement) in Zenkutsu-Dachi

(for explanation see next page)

Explanation on Sukui-Uke

A Mae-Geri attack is blocked, held by a scooping movement and thrown to the side

Transition and recovery into Shuto-Uke. The left foot is placed vertical to the left shoulder below the solar plexus. Then pull forward to the right in Kokutsu-Dachi

Step forward in Kokutsu-Dachi with a right Shuto-Uke

Left Sukui-Uke in Zenkutsu-Dachi. Fix your gaze on a point about 4 metres ahead during both defensive movements

Explanation:

90° transition in Kokutsu-Dachi, using Shuto-Uke deflection

90° transition in Kokutsu-Dachi, with right Shuto-Uke.
Note: Look in opposite direction! Make sure only the head is turned the other way

Other form: Right Tate-Shuto-Uke in Kokutsu-Dachi

Explanation:

Another way of explaining the move: the opponent is held with Tate-Shuto-Uke and pushed to the side during the transition movement

Converting from right Kokutsu-Dachi to left Kokutsu-Dachi: there are 3 possible forms: the usual form is stepping across

Third form (Japanese, not illustrated): place the foot in direct line with the solar plexus, without closing the feet

Kanazawa form: when closing the feet, straighten up, then step into the position with a powerful twist of the hips

Shuto-Uke in Kokutsu-Dachi with Kiai!

Closing position of Bassai-Dai Kata

From here, move the right foot away into the closing position in Hachiji-Dachi with Shizentai

159

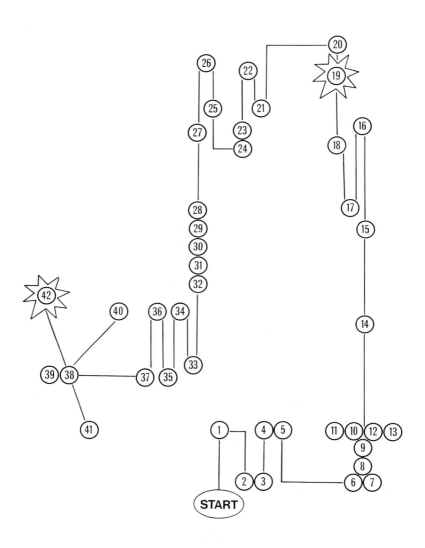

Step-by-step diagram of the 7th
Kata sequence (for explanation,
see 1st Kata, page 23)

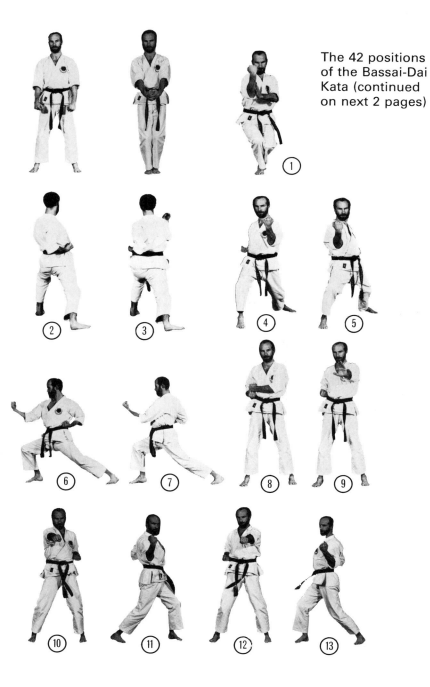

The 42 positions of the Bassai-Dai Kata (continued on next 2 pages)

161

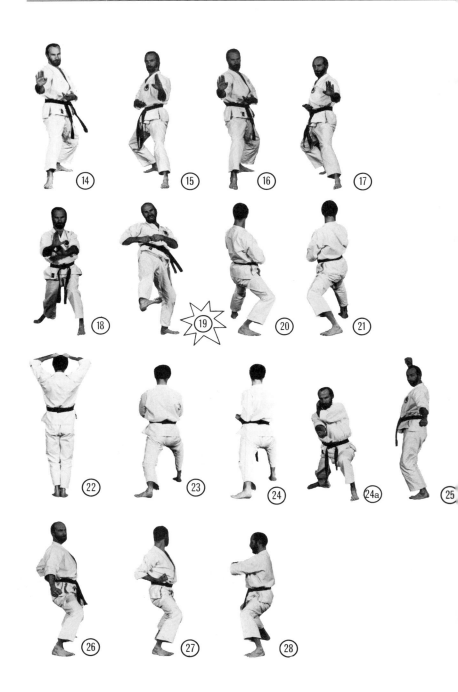

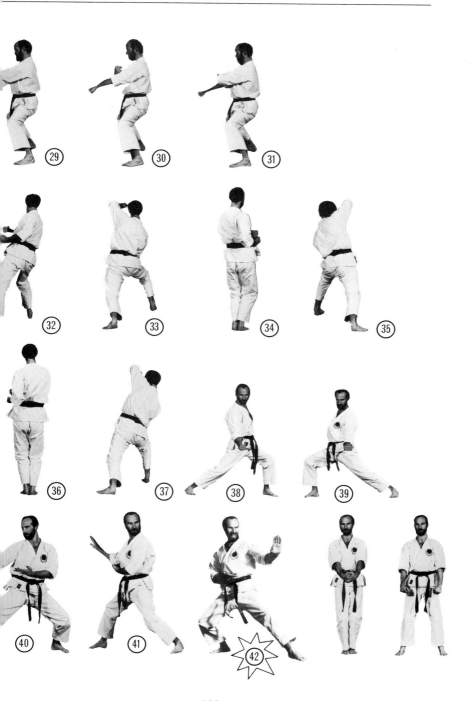

CONCLUSION

If you have learned all the Kata sequences in this book, you will have taken a giant step forward towards complete mastery of the art. But it is important to realise that, in Karate, learning is a continual process. Even a master never ceases to learn, continuing to hone and polish Kata performance, regardless of whether this is basic or more advanced Kata form.

Time and again, the Karateka will measure progress by the clarity of line in performance. If the lines are not clean and precise (and unfortunately this is all too often the case), the meaning and purpose of Karate will be lost, especially in the light of comparison with the uncompromising nature and power of intensive Karate study.

With every good wish for your success!

Wolf-Dieter Wichmann